WITHDRAWN

The Living WORLD

SCIENCE
UP
CLOSE

APOLLO MEMORIAL LIBRARY
219 N. PENNSYLVANIA AVE.
APOLLO, PA 15613

Science Photo Library

JULIAN
MESSNER

PHOTO CREDITS

Doug Allan p. 3; David Leah p. 4; Jan Hinsch p. 5; Sinclair Stammers pp. 6, 16(T.), 20; Jeremy Burgess p. 6(R.), 7, 8, 11(2), 12(B.), 13, 19(2), 23(B.); Jonathan Watts p. 9; Claude Nuridsany and Marie Perennou p. 10; David Scharf pp. 12(T.), 21(T.); Cath Wadforth, Department of Zoology, University of Hull pp. 14, 15, 23(T.); David Spears p. 16(B.); T. E. Thompson p. 17; Keith Ruffell p. 18; Darwin Dale p. 21(B.); Tony Brain p. 22(2); Eric Gravé pp. 24, 28; John Walsh p. 25; Manfred Kage pp. 26, 29 (T.); C. Chumbley p. 27; Martin Dohrn pp. 29(B.), 31; R. Clark and M. Goff p. 30; Petit Format, Nestlé p. 32.

Copyright © 1990 by Julian Messner. First published by Young Library Ltd., Brighton, England. Copyright © 1988 Young Library Ltd. Photos courtesy Science Photo Library, Ltd. All rights reserved including the right of reproduction in whole or in part in any form. Published by Julian Messner, a division of Silver Burdett Press, Inc., Simon & Schuster, Inc., Prentice Hall Bldg., Englewood Cliffs, NJ 07632. JULIAN MESSNER and colophon are trademarks of Simon & Schuster, Inc. Design by R Studio T. Manufactured in the United States of America.

Lib. ed. 10 9 8 7 6 5 4 3 2 1
Paper ed. 10 9 8 7 6 5 4 3 2 1

Library of Congress Cataloging-in-Publication Data
Cleeve, Roger.
[Beautiful life]
The living world/by Roger Cleeve.
p. cm.—(Science up close)
Reprint. Originally published: Beautiful life. Brighton, England: Young Library, c1988.
Summary: A microscopic look at some of the wonders of nature.
1. Animals—Pictorial works—Juvenile literature. 2. Plants —Pictorial works—Juvenile literature. [1. Animals. 2. Plants.]
I. Title. II. Series.
QL49.C63 1990
ISBN 0-671-68627-5 ISBN 0-671-68630-5 (pbk.)
574—dc20   89-29316
                                                            CIP
                                                             AC

A spider has spun an orb web. The fine threads carry a sticky substance that will capture the spider's prey.

This is one of the largest of all plants. It is a cypress tree in Mexico. Its trunk is so thick that you would need about half a minute to walk around it. It drinks in enough water through its roots each day to fill a small swimming pool.

The strange and colorful shapes opposite are also plants. However, they are about as different from trees as it is possible to be. They are tiny, microscopic plants called diatoms. They float about in water. A single cupful of sea water can contain several thousand of them.

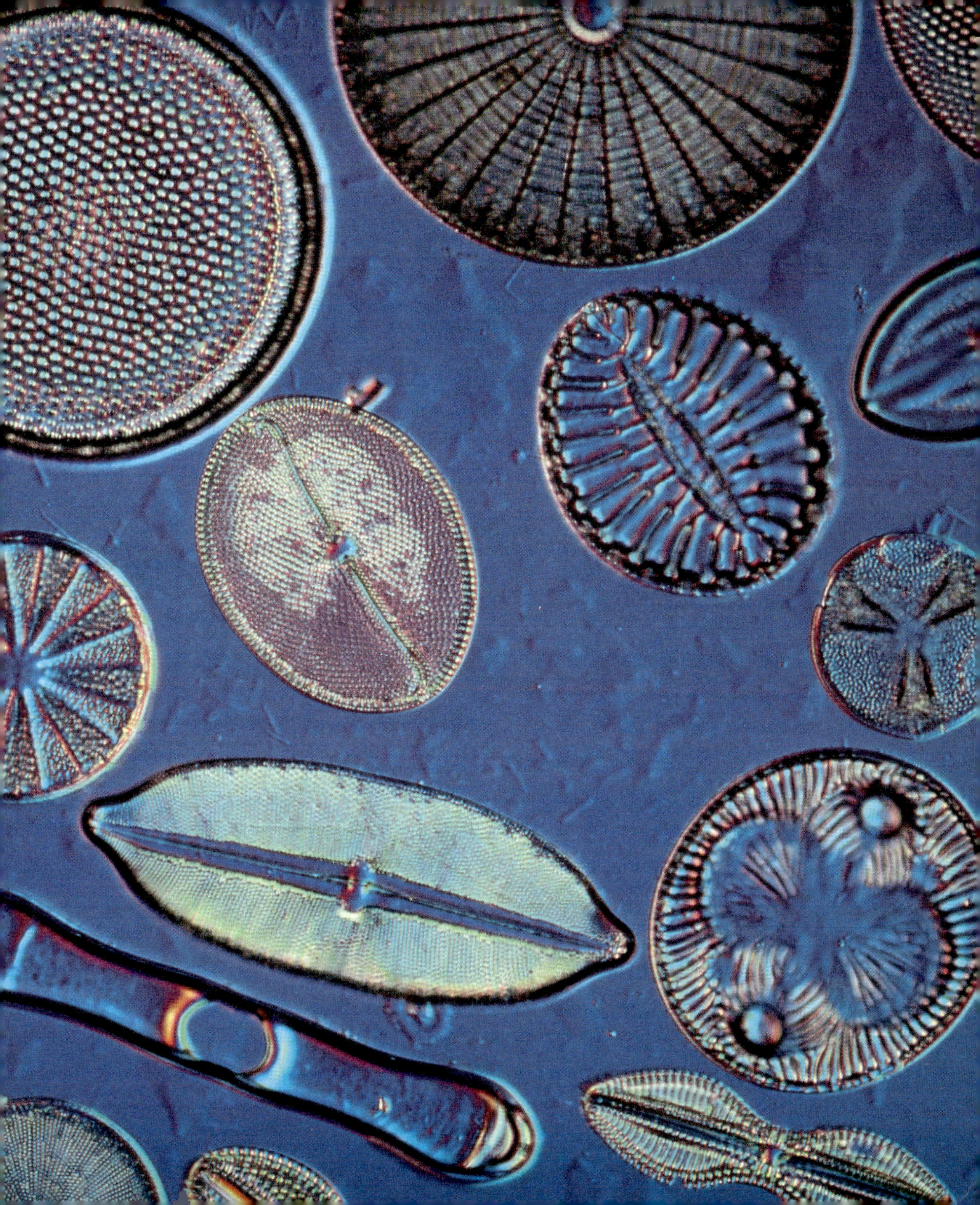

6

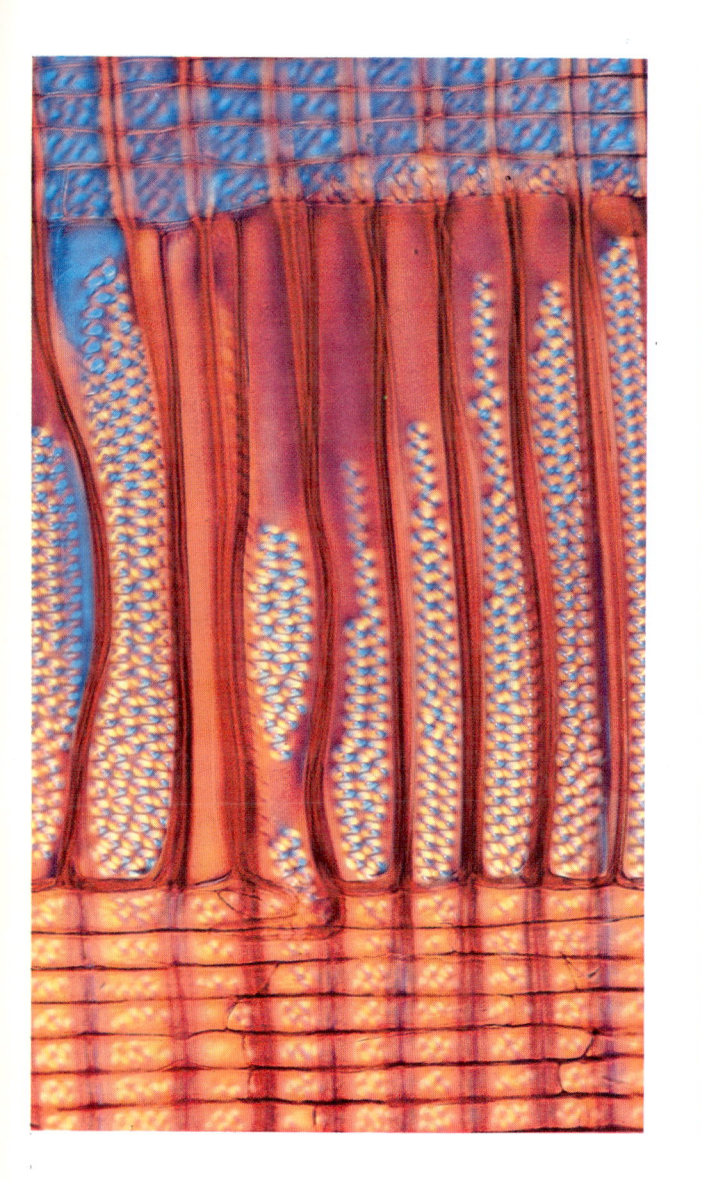

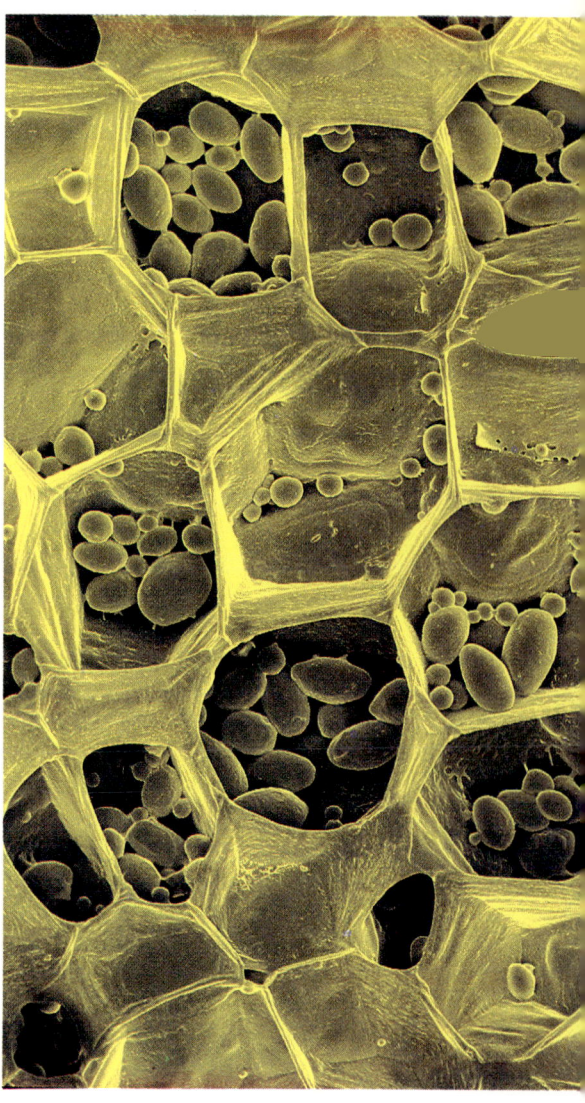

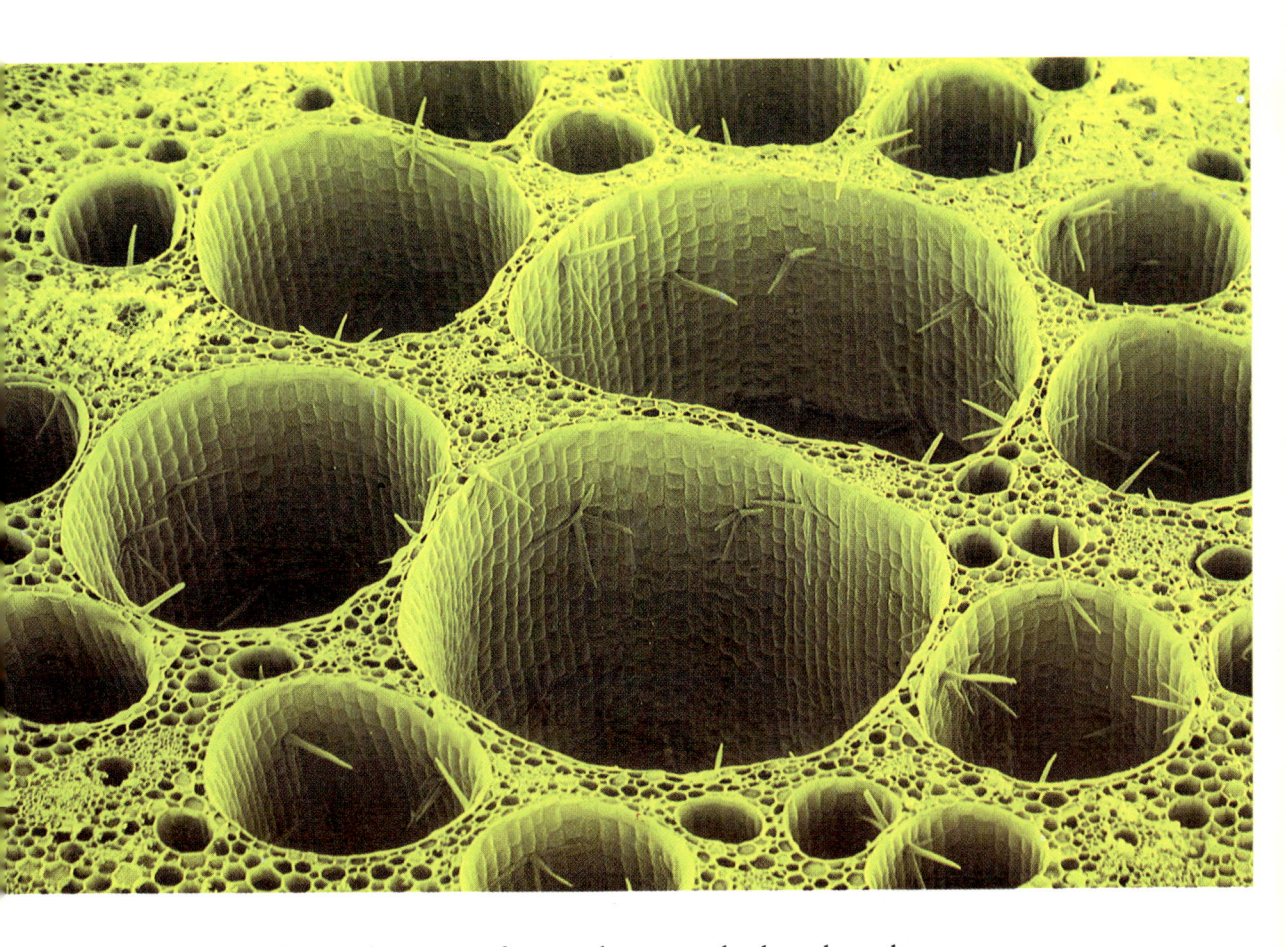

Here are three slices cut from plants and placed under a microscope. On the far left is a section of tree trunk. The vertical, or up-and-down, lines are tubes that draw up water from the roots. The second picture shows a section of potato. You can see egg-shaped grains of starch inside the cells. The photo above shows a section of water-lily stalk. The round tubes carry air from the leaves, which are above water, down to the roots below.

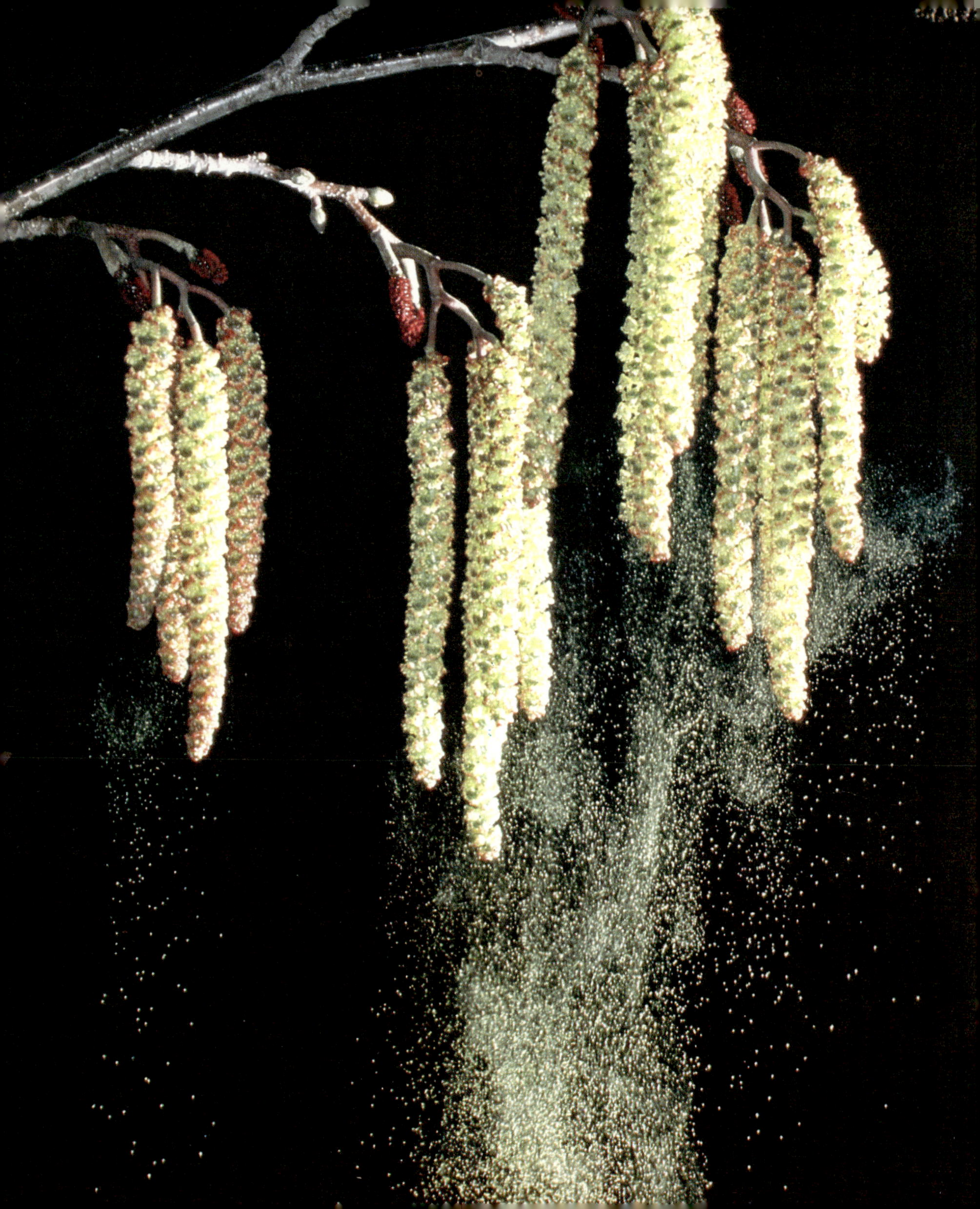

In the picture opposite, a slight breeze has shaken the yellow, dustlike pollen from a drooping catkin, or flower, on an alder tree. The pollen will drift in the air, perhaps for days. Pollen from "male" flowers or flower parts must settle on "female" ones to produce seeds that can later germinate, or sprout.

Wind can carry and spread seeds. The photo above shows seeds being blown off a dandelion. They are much heavier than pollen. You can see that they have little "parachutes" to help them travel farther in the air before they settle.

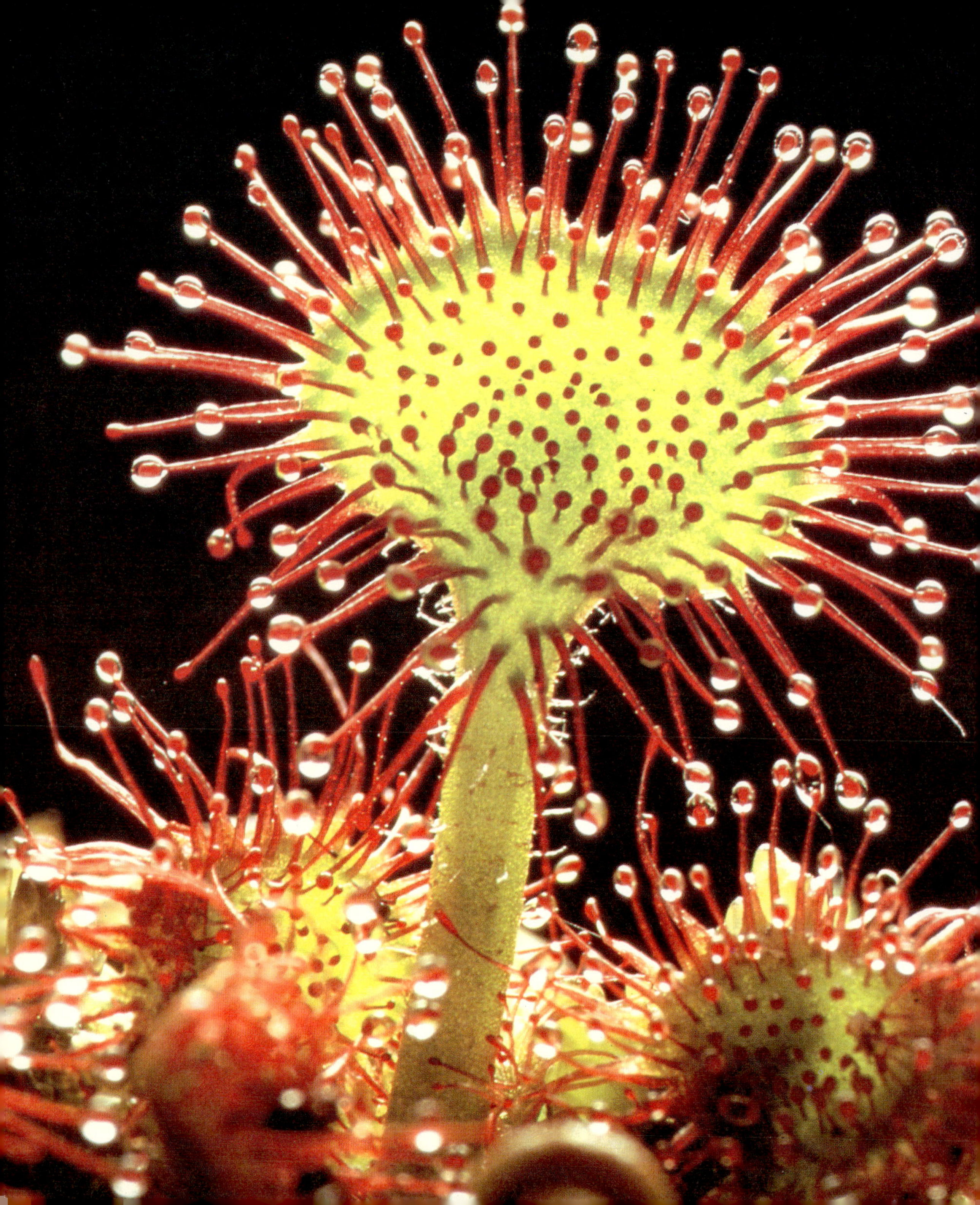

The sundew plant, opposite, grows in flooded bogs or swamps, where it cannot get enough nitrogen from soil. Instead, it gets its nitrogen from insects. It catches them on the ends of its long, sticky tentacles. Then it digests the insects.

The leaves and stem of the stinging nettle (right) are covered with hairs. Some of the hairs are like tiny hypodermic needles. The slightest touch of a finger causes the little bulb at the tip to break off. The hair tip then shoots a stinging liquid into the skin.

Below you can see flower parts of a grass called Cocksfoot. The pinkish, drooping parts are called anthers. They produce pollen.

To the right is a marigold petal, viewed through a microscope. The petal would look smooth to your unaided eye, but as you can see, it is patterned with ridges.

Below is a microscope photo of a sepal, or leaflike structure, at the base of a lavender flower. The lavender sepal has oil glands on its surfaces. The little balls of fragrant oil these glands produce nestle among branched hairs. Next time you smell lavender perfume, you will know where its scent comes from.

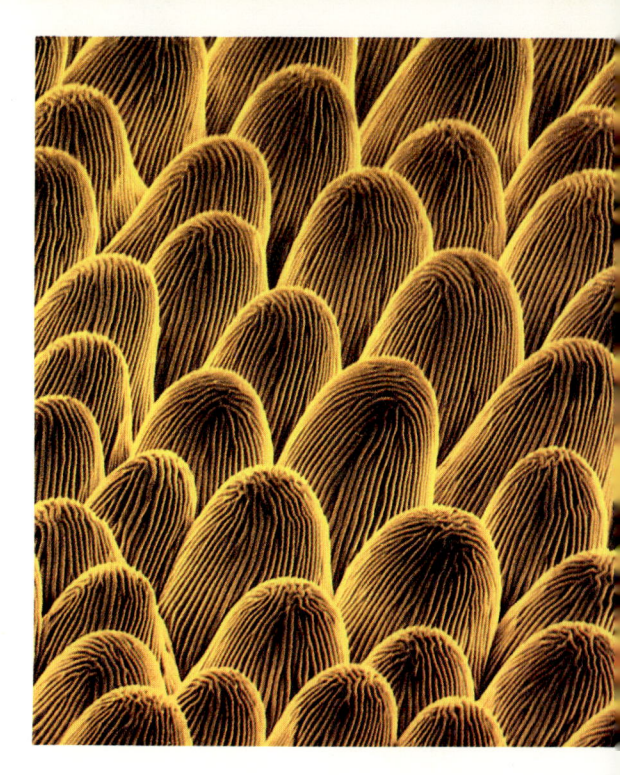

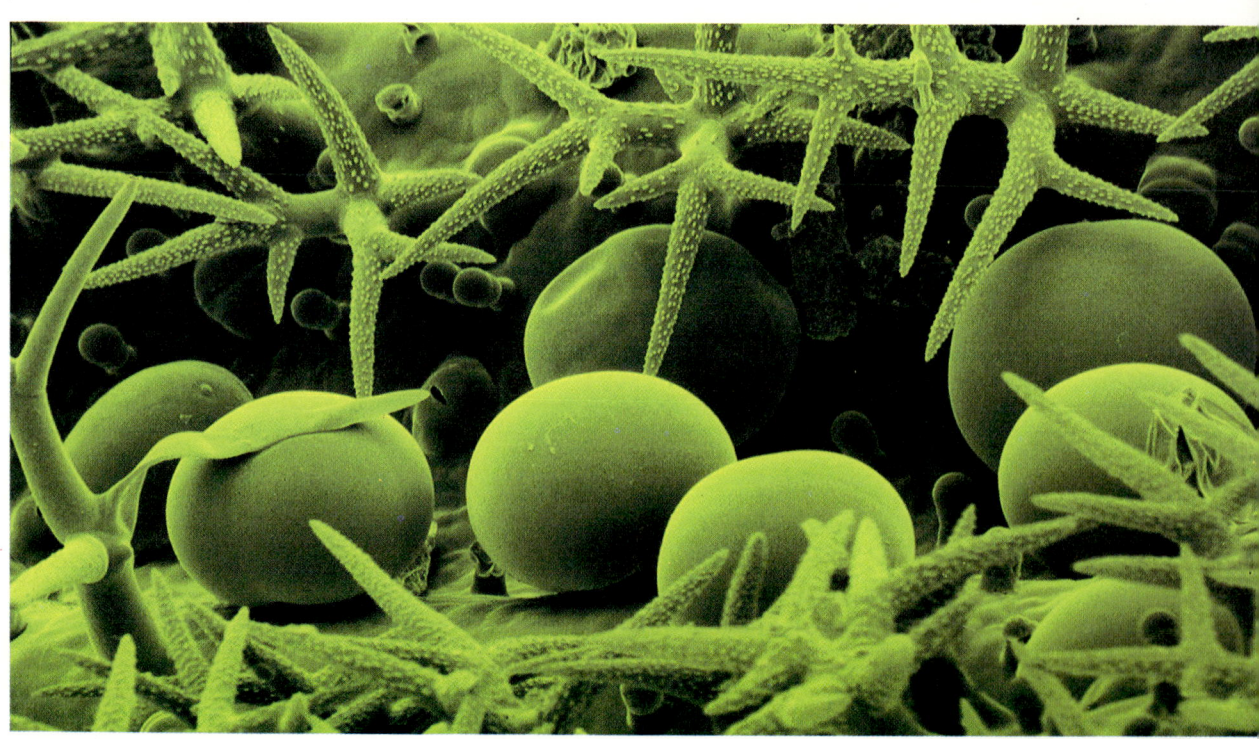

The yeasts above are very different from marigold and lavender. Yeasts are not green plants, but funguses. They are so tiny that hundreds of them would fit on a pinhead. Yeasts can produce alcohol and carbon dioxide gas. The alcohol is used in making beer and wine. The carbon dioxide is used in breadmaking. The yeast forces little bubbles of the gas into bread dough. That makes the dough swell and become light and airy.

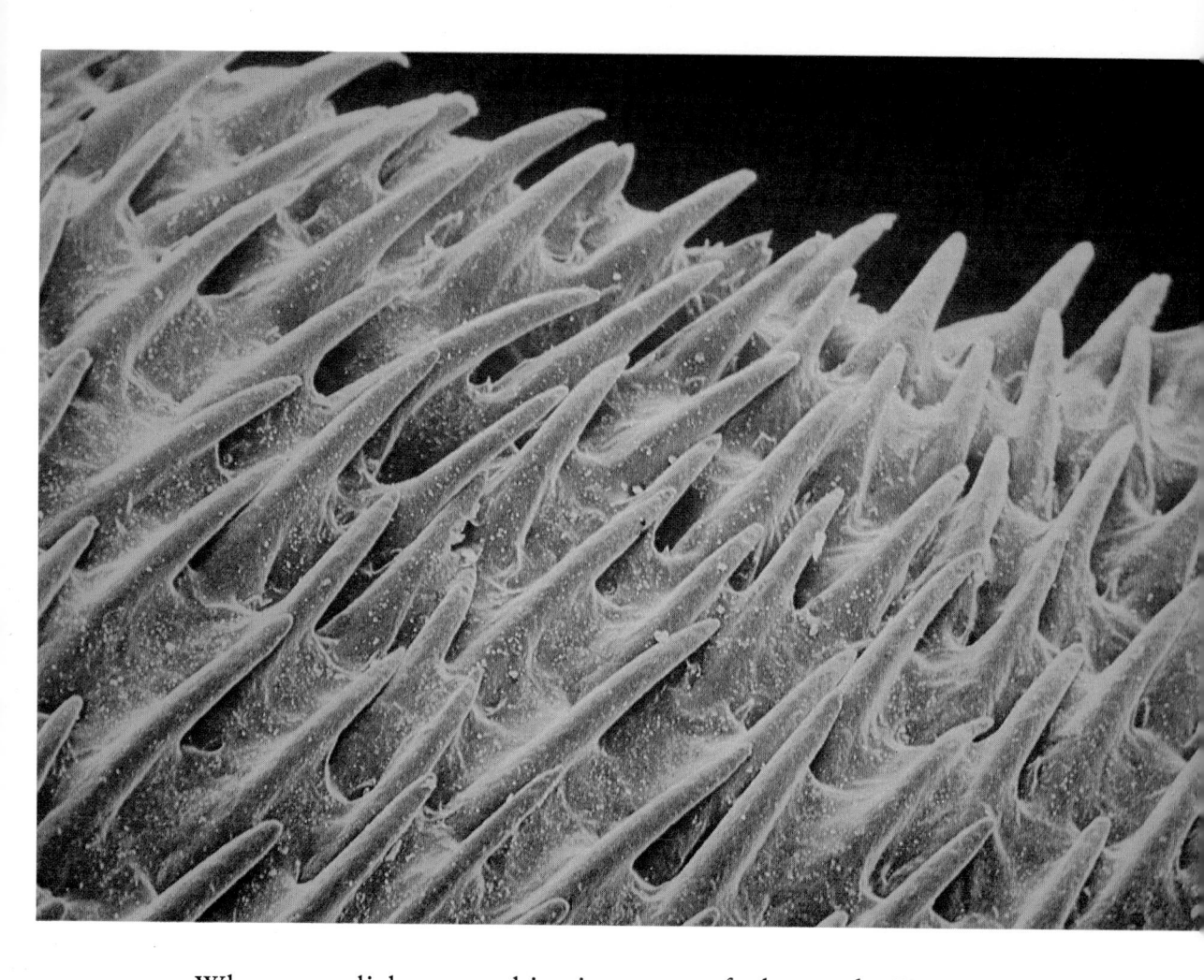

When a cat licks your skin, its tongue feels rough. Here you can see why. The tongue has spikes on it. When a cat licks its fur, it is not only washing it but also combing it. The spikes are useful for lapping up liquids, too. The liquid is scooped up in the pits between the spikes.

Above is a close-up picture of a flea. You may have heard a rhyme about fleas that goes:

*Great fleas have little fleas upon their backs to bite 'em,
And little fleas have lesser fleas, and so ad infinitum.*

By looking at the picture, you can see that the rhyme is right, in a way. The back of the hedgehog flea is covered with scales. Just under the scales, you can see white, spiderlike mites. The mites use suckers on their feet to cling to the flea.

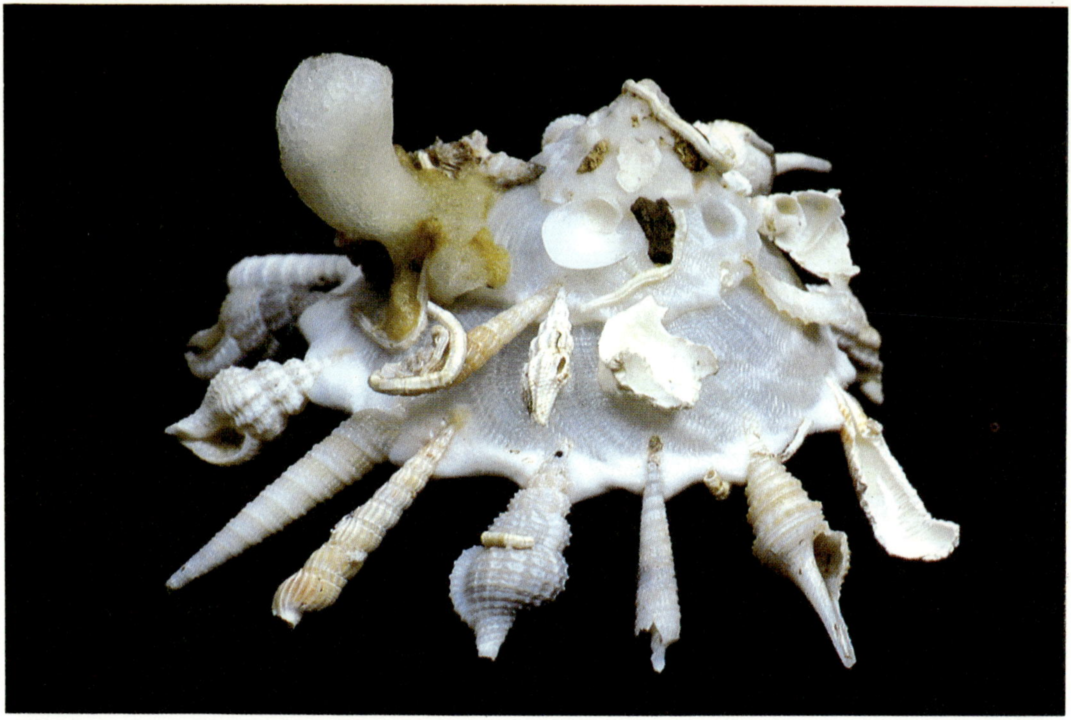

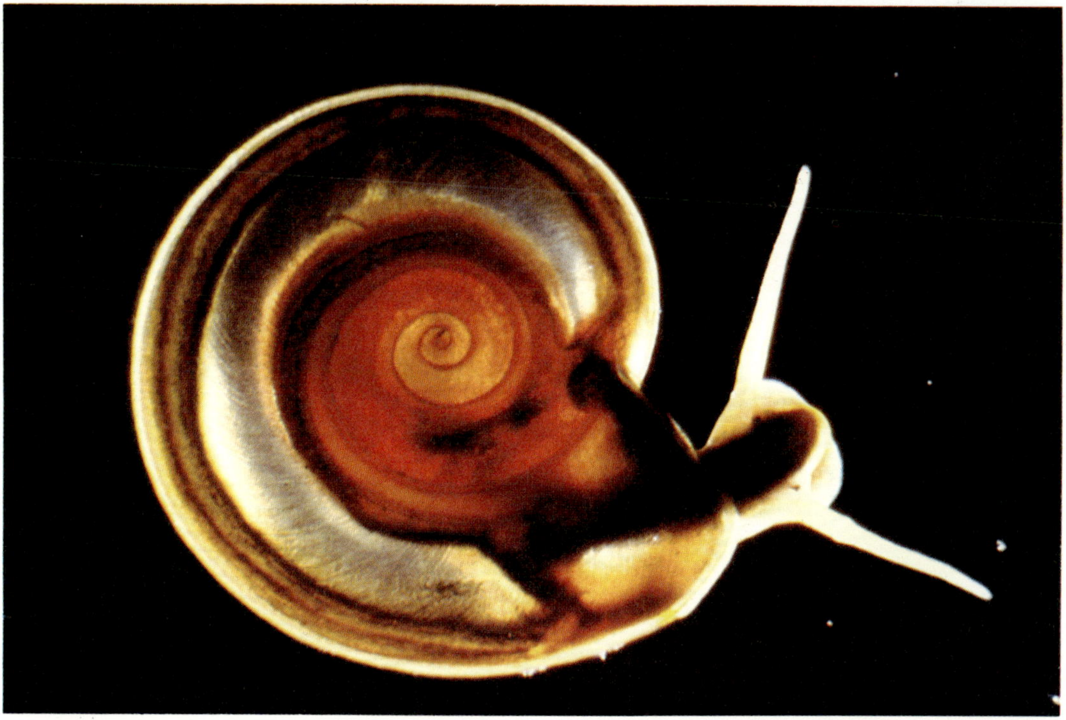

Opposite, above, you see a creature called a carrier shellfish. It attaches empty shells to its own shell with a gluelike material. By doing this, it protects itself. An enemy looking for food would probably attack one of the empty shells instead of the carrier shellfish.

Opposite, below, is another water creature that has a shell. This Button Ramshorn snail has a shell that is thin and flat. In this photograph, light is shining right through the shell. You can see the long, thin, whitish snail's body inside.

The frilly creature below is a sea slug that lives in the Caribbean Sea. You are seeing it from underneath. It travels by making wavy movements in the water.

This Brimstone butterfly is feeding on sweet-pea flowers. Flowers like the sweet pea have a honeylike liquid, called nectar, that insects like to eat.

The photo above shows how butterflies are able to get at nectar. You are seeing the butterfly's head, one of its eyes, and one antenna. The black, curved shape to the left is the butterfly's rolled-up tongue. The insect feeds by uncoiling the tongue and dipping it deep into the flower.

This picture shows a cluster of butterfly eggs. A newly hatched, wormlike caterpillar has just come out of one of them. The caterpillar will later wrap itself in a cocoonlike chrysalis shell. Later still, it will come out of the chrysalis in the form of a flying adult butterfly.

Above is a millipede, curled into a tight spiral on a leaf. Millipedes have two pairs of legs on most of their body segments. In spite of all the legs, millipedes cannot run fast.

The creatures opposite, above, are aphids. Ants love them because the aphids produce a sweet substance. But farmers and gardeners hate the aphids because these insects destroy plants. The aphids do this by sucking sap and by spreading plant diseases. When it is time to move to a fresh plant, the winged female aphids float on air currents for several hours. They can climb to heights of about a third of a mile before coming down again.

Below the aphids is a creature called a fruit fly. There are 2,000 species, or types, of fruit fly. Some of them are so alike, you might wonder how a female fruit fly can make sure she mates only with a male of her own species. She listens to the buzzing noise made by the males' wings. All members of a species buzz at the same pitch. The pitch is different for different species.

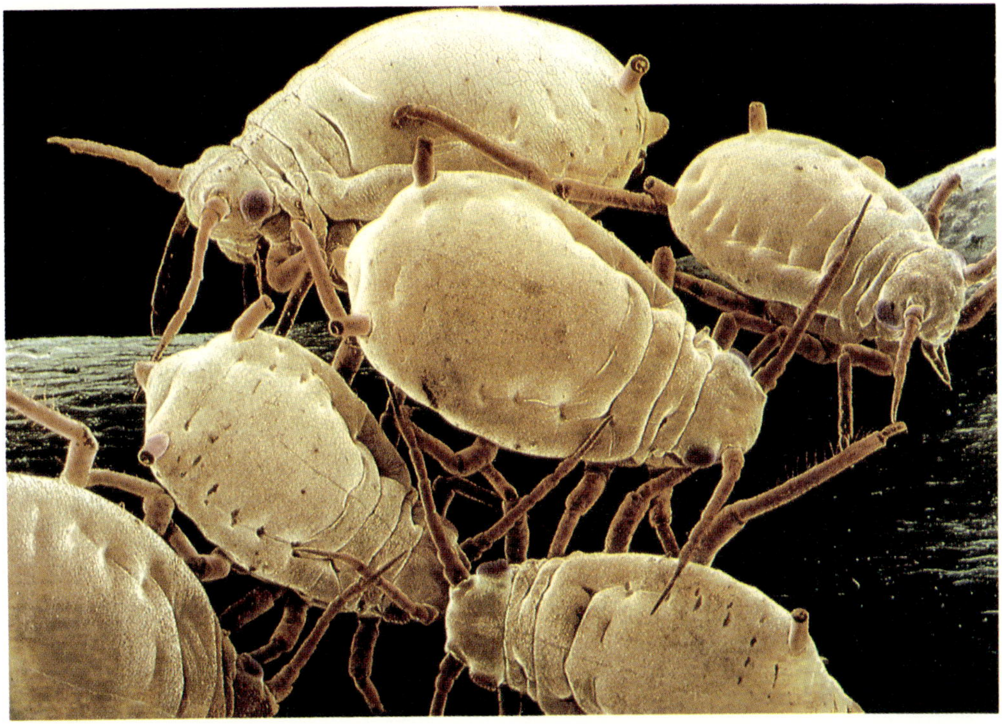

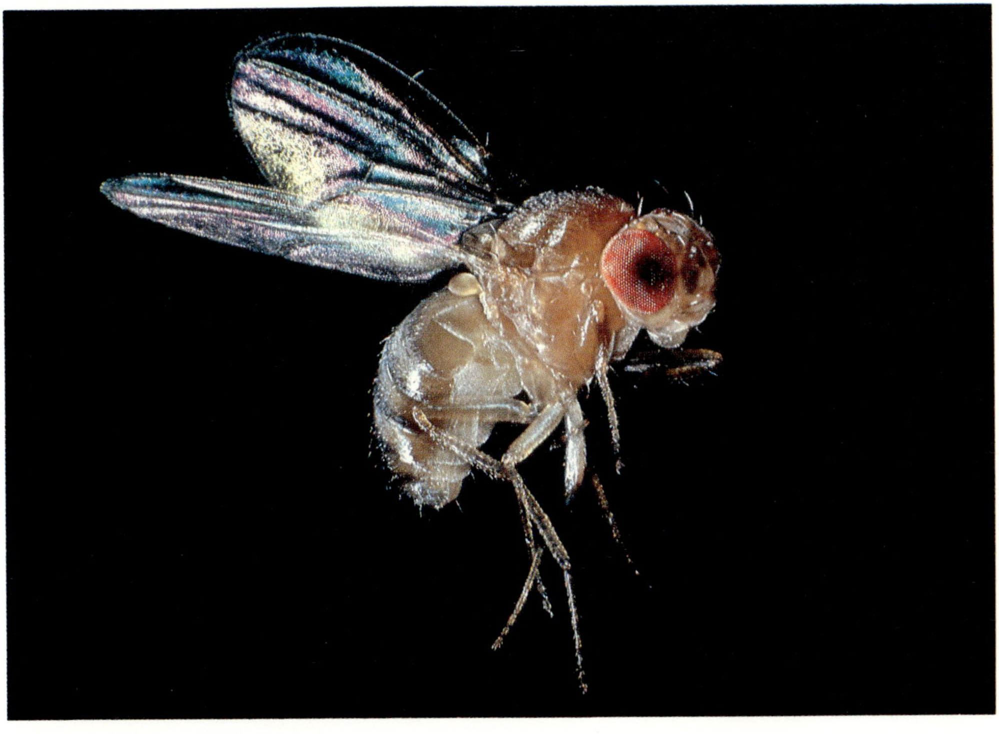

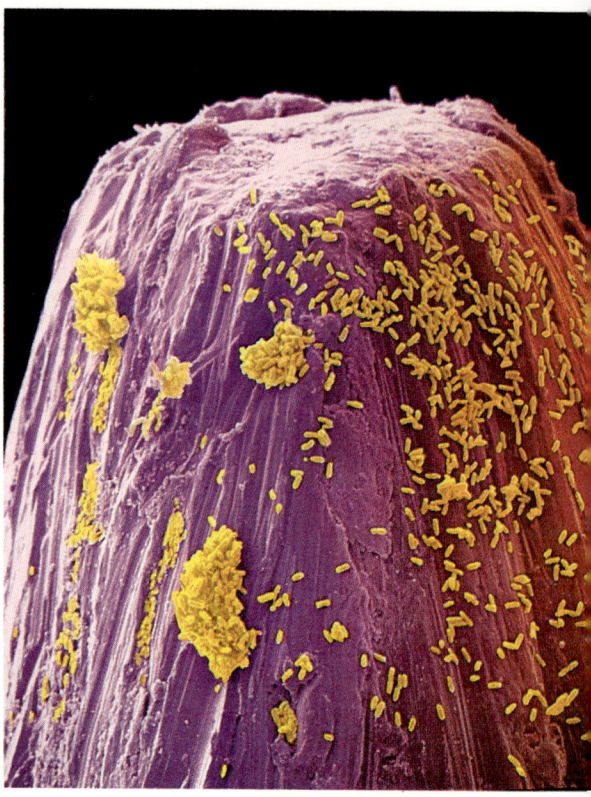

On the left is a pinpoint, about 24 times the real size. On the right is the *same* pinpoint magnified 600 times. You can now see thousands of little yellow blobs. These are living creatures called bacteria. Bacteria live everywhere, including the inside of every animal—even inside you!

Bees (opposite, below) visit flowers to collect nectar. They store it in the hive as food for the winter. You can see the bee's long "tongue" poking deep into the flower to reach the nectar. Pollen from the flower sticks to the orange "basket" on the bee's back knee, and is carried back to the hive.

At right is something that looks like a helmeted warrior from another world. This fearsome-looking creature is really part of a tiny tapeworm. Tapeworms live inside the bodies of animals. They feed on the digested food inside the animals. The umbrella-shaped structure you see is a hook, and the two eye-shaped structures are large suckers. The tapeworm uses these to attach itself to the inside of the animals. The tapeworm shown here lives inside a sea creature called a barnacle.

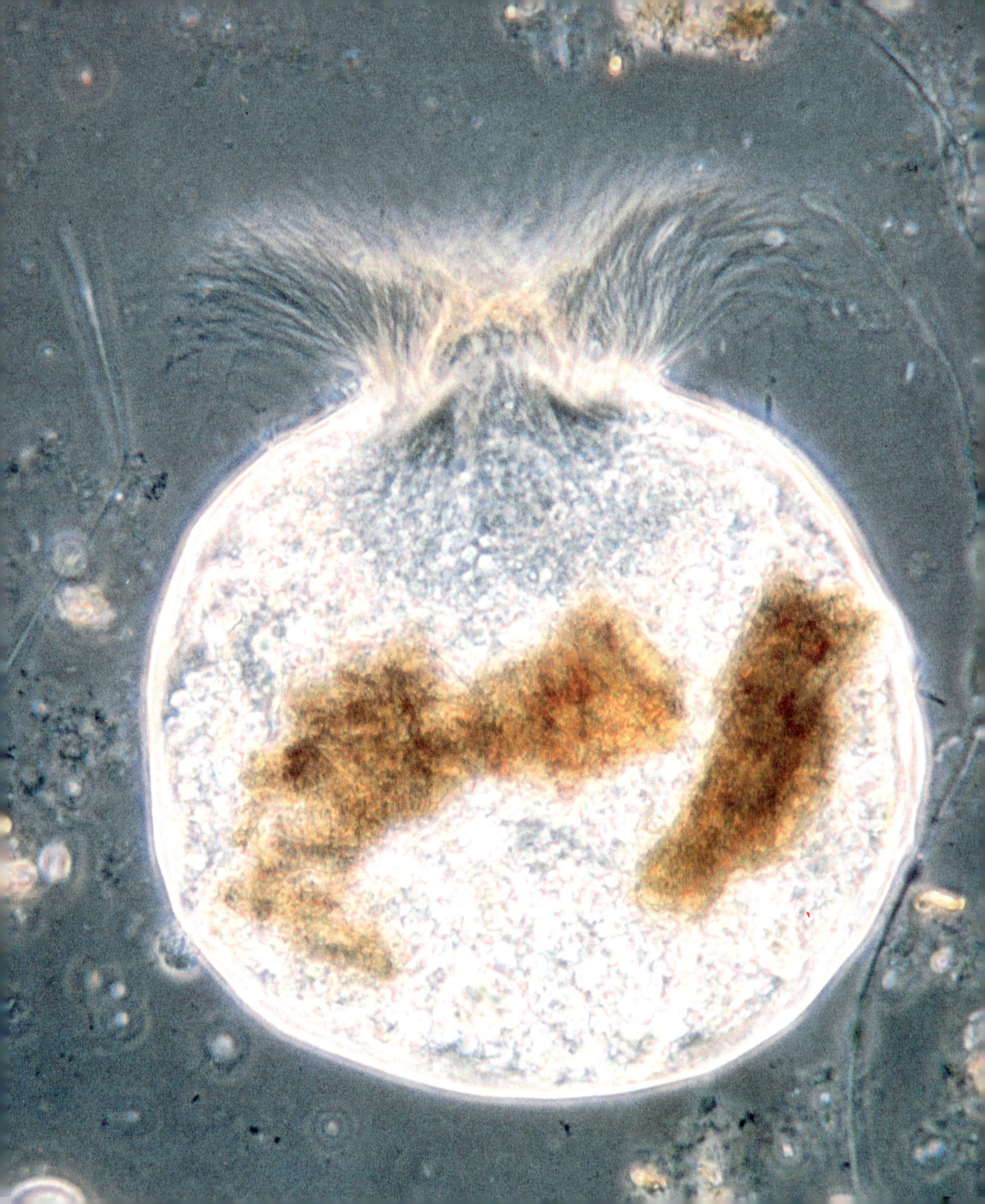

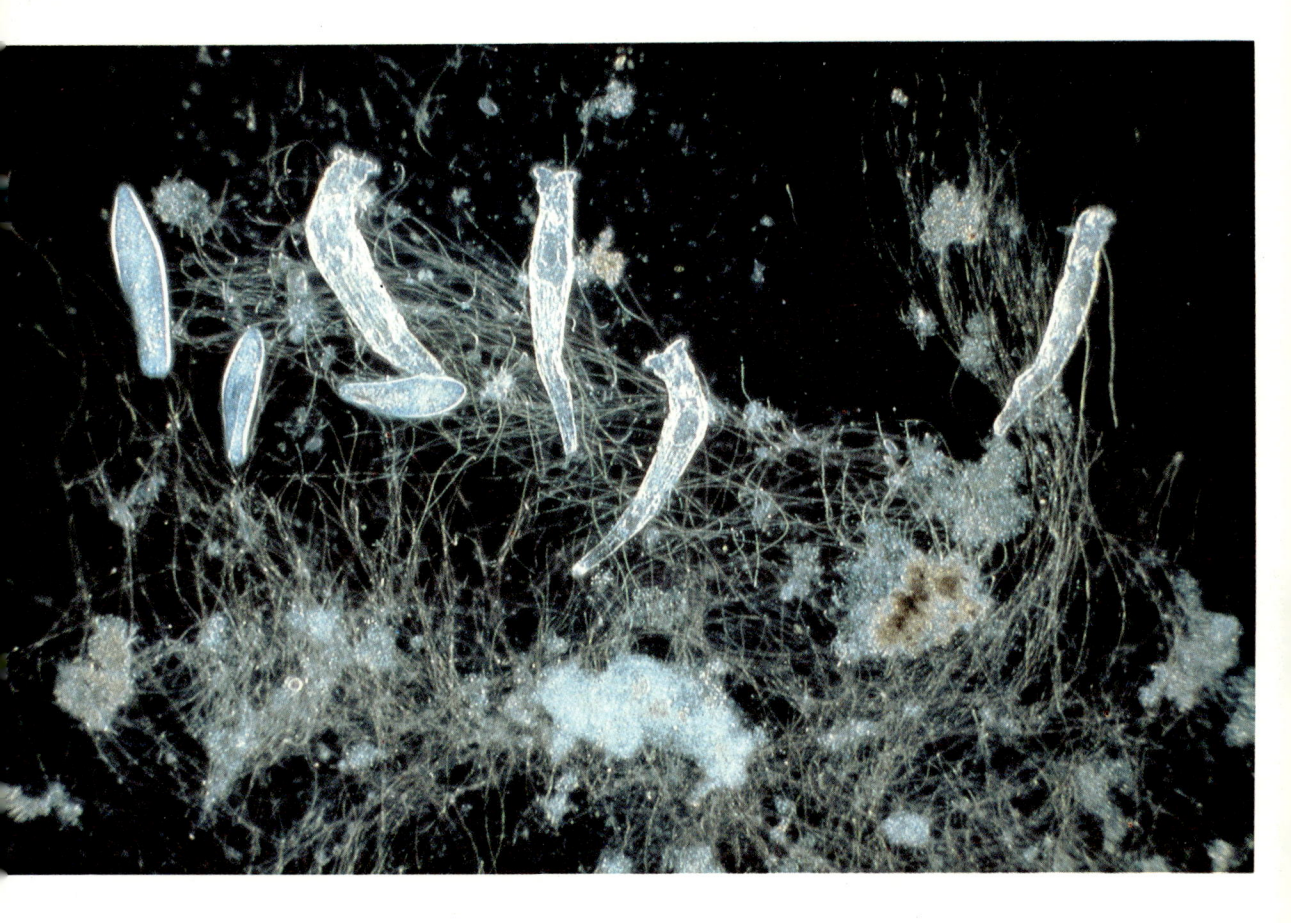

Above is a picture of rotifers. Almost any fresh water contains these little dancing creatures. The largest of them are only about 1/16-inch long. They are transparent, or clear, so you can see the organs inside them. They move by beating the water with tiny hairs that surround their mouths.

The protozoan shown opposite lives inside a wood-eating cockroach. Unlike the tapeworm, it helps rather than harms its host. It allows the cockroach to digest wood. Neither creature could live without the other.

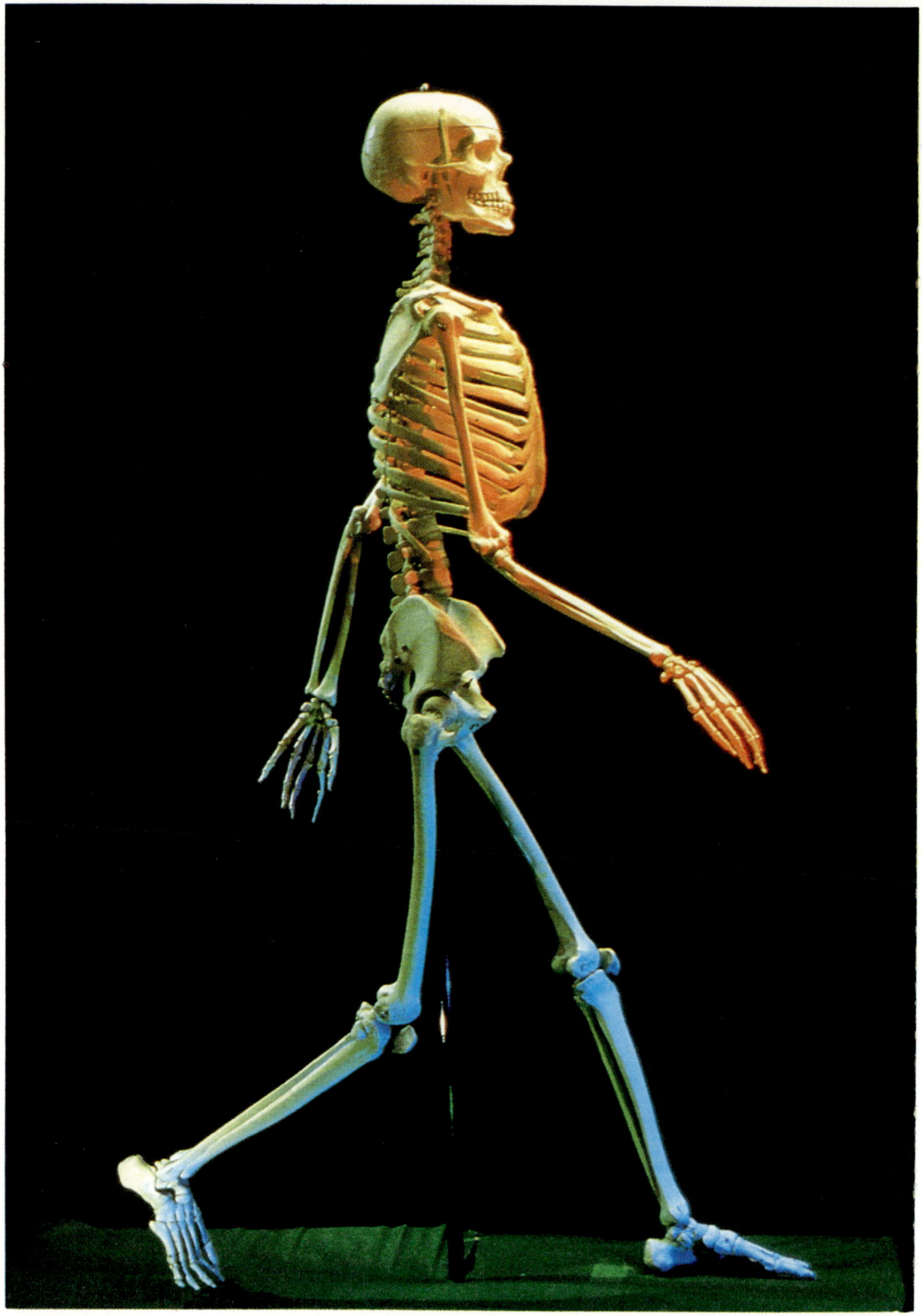

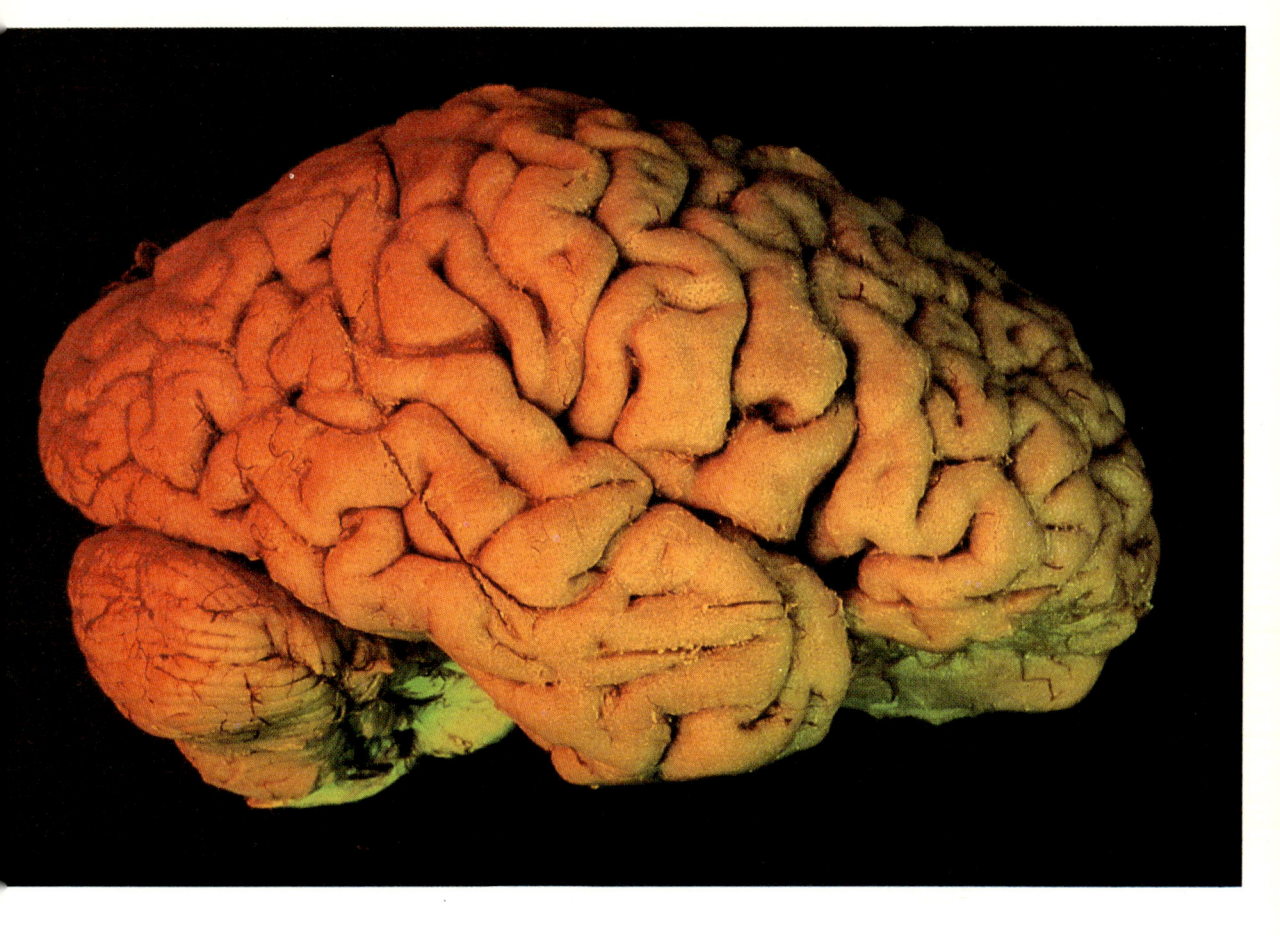

Opposite, you see the bones of one of the strangest creatures in this book—an apelike creature that walks on two legs. It is a human. The bony skeleton is the framework for the body. It holds the body upright. It also supports muscles and protects the inner organs.

The lump of wrinkled jelly, above, is the smartest computer ever made. It is a human brain. Each brain has about 14 billion nerve cells. That is nearly three times the number of people there are on Earth. If you are more than six years old, your brain is already about as big as it is ever going to be.

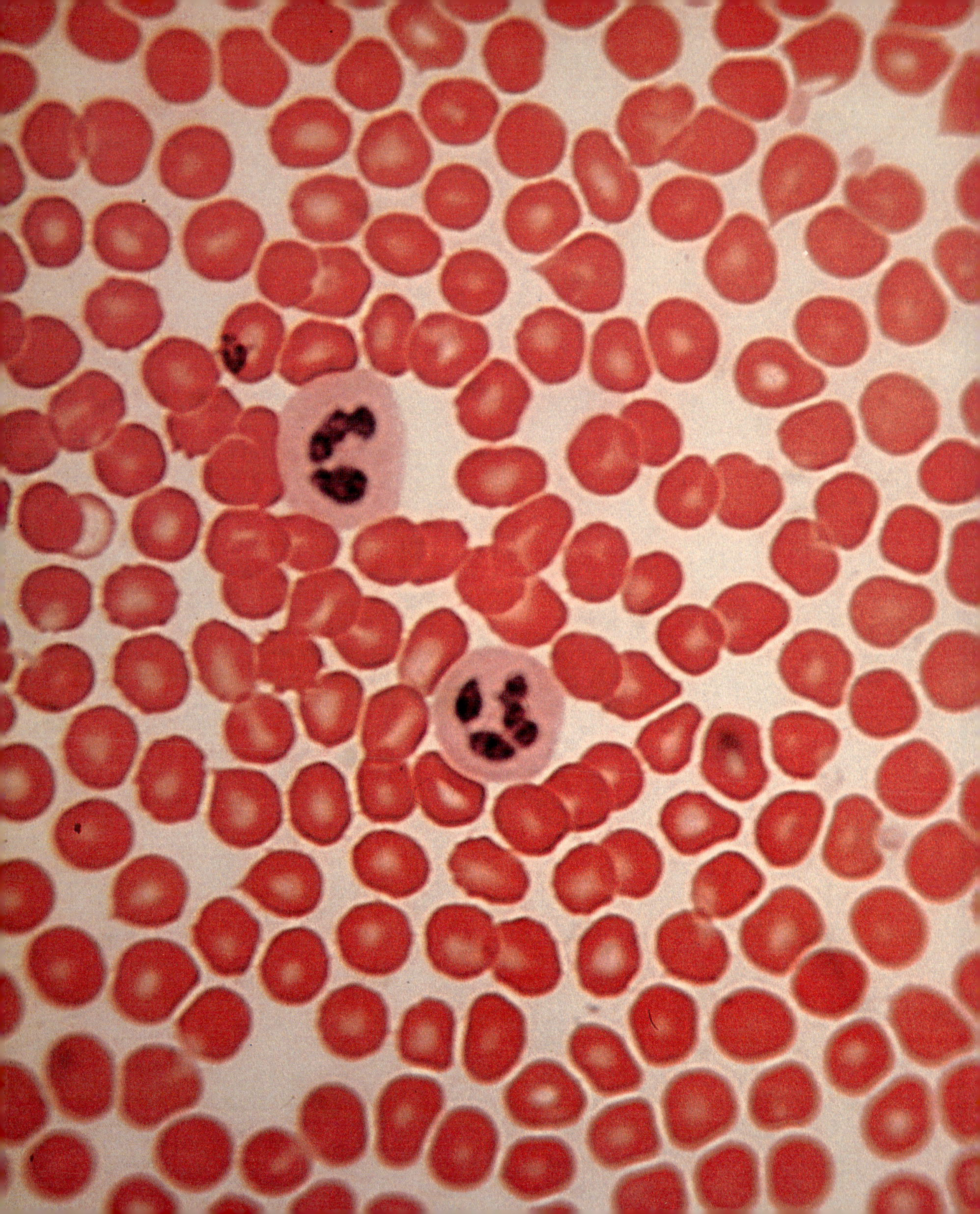

When you cut yourself, you see a red liquid. However, when seen under a microscope (left), blood is really a pale liquid with lumps, called cells, in it. Most of the cells are red. They carry oxygen through the body. Most of the rest of the cells are pinkish white. They help to fight disease. In this smear of human blood, you can see two of these white cells.

The two pictures on this page show the blood supply to the head (top) and the lungs (below). Blood flows through the narrow networks of tubes. These tubes are called veins, capillaries, and arteries. There are 35,000 miles of them in the body. That is enough to stretch one-and-a-half times around the world.

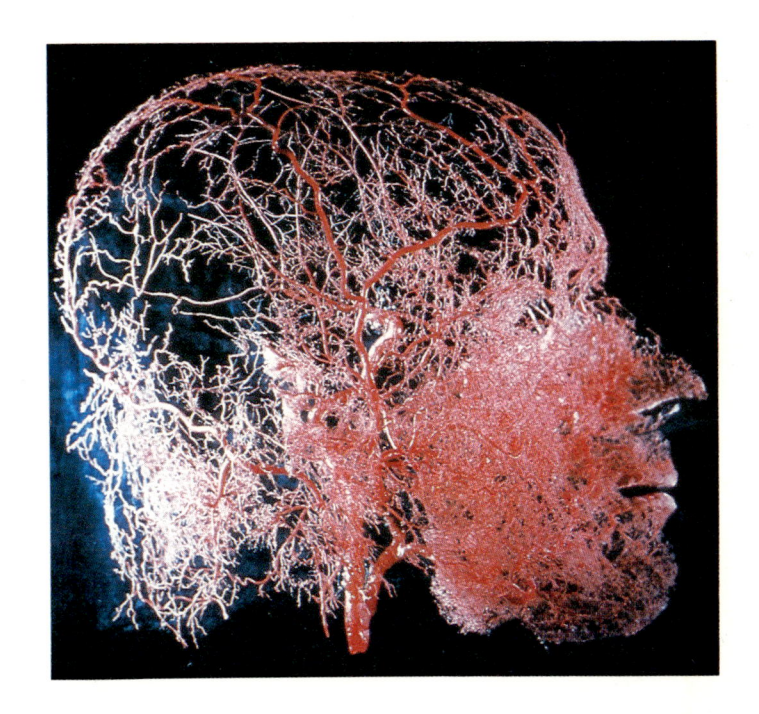

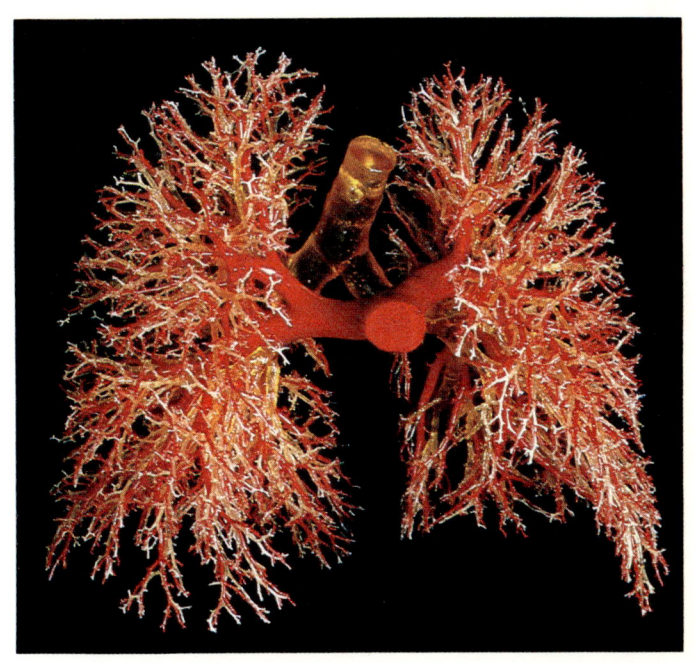

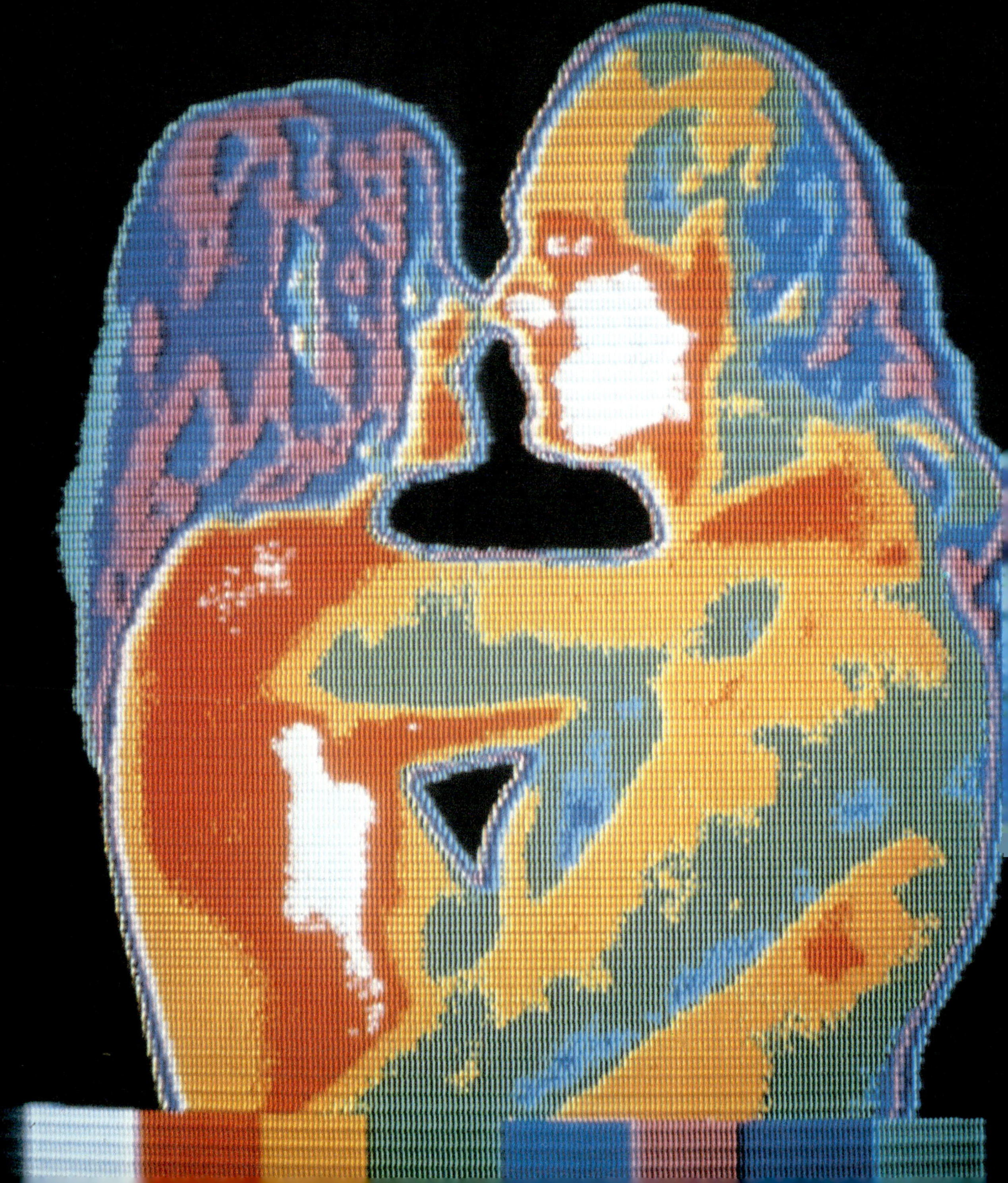

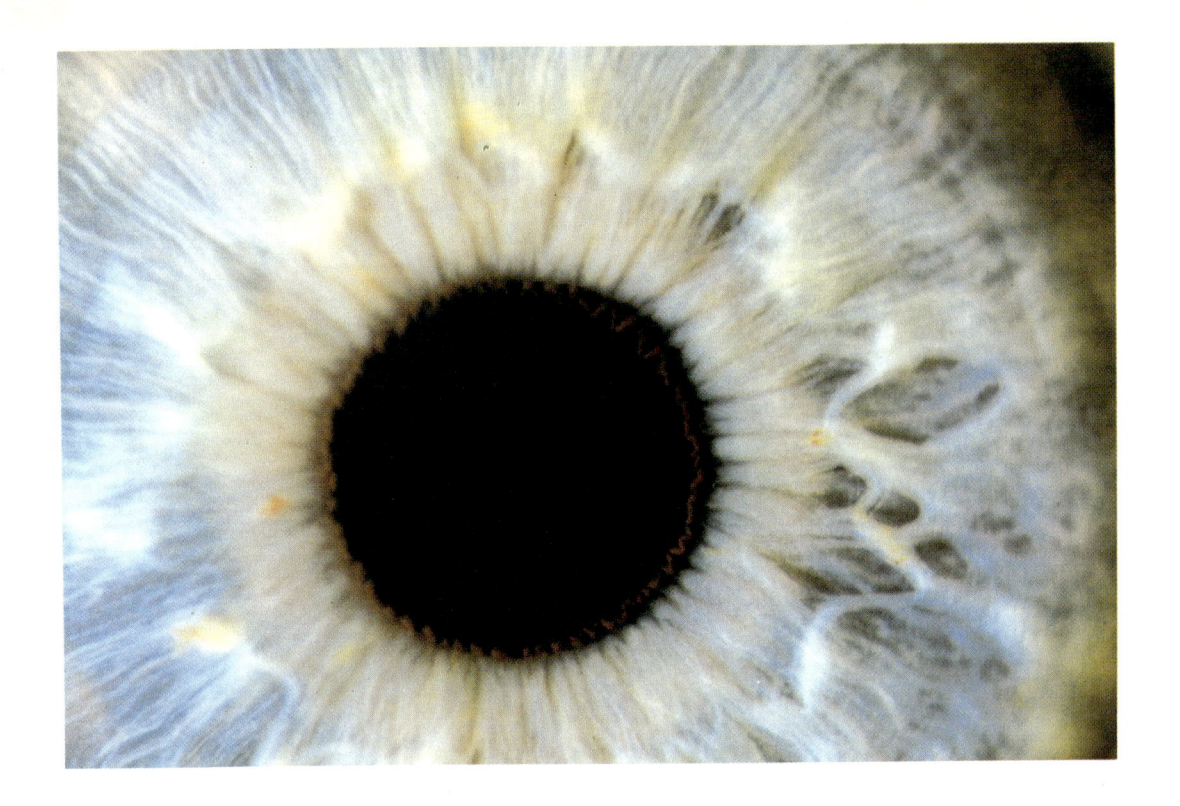

Opposite is a thermograph, a picture that is taken using heat instead of light. It shows that skin is not the same temperature all over the body. In this picture of a couple hugging, the white areas are the warmest, the blues and greens are the coolest. The woman's head does not appear as warm as the man's because it is covered with cold hair. Can you guess why the man's head looks warmer at the front than at the back?

The human eye (above) is very sensitive to light. The picture shows the black pupil surrounded by the blue iris. In darkness, the pupil opens wide to let in as much light as possible. This photo was taken using a flashbulb. The flash made the pupil shrink to pinpoint size a split second after it went off.

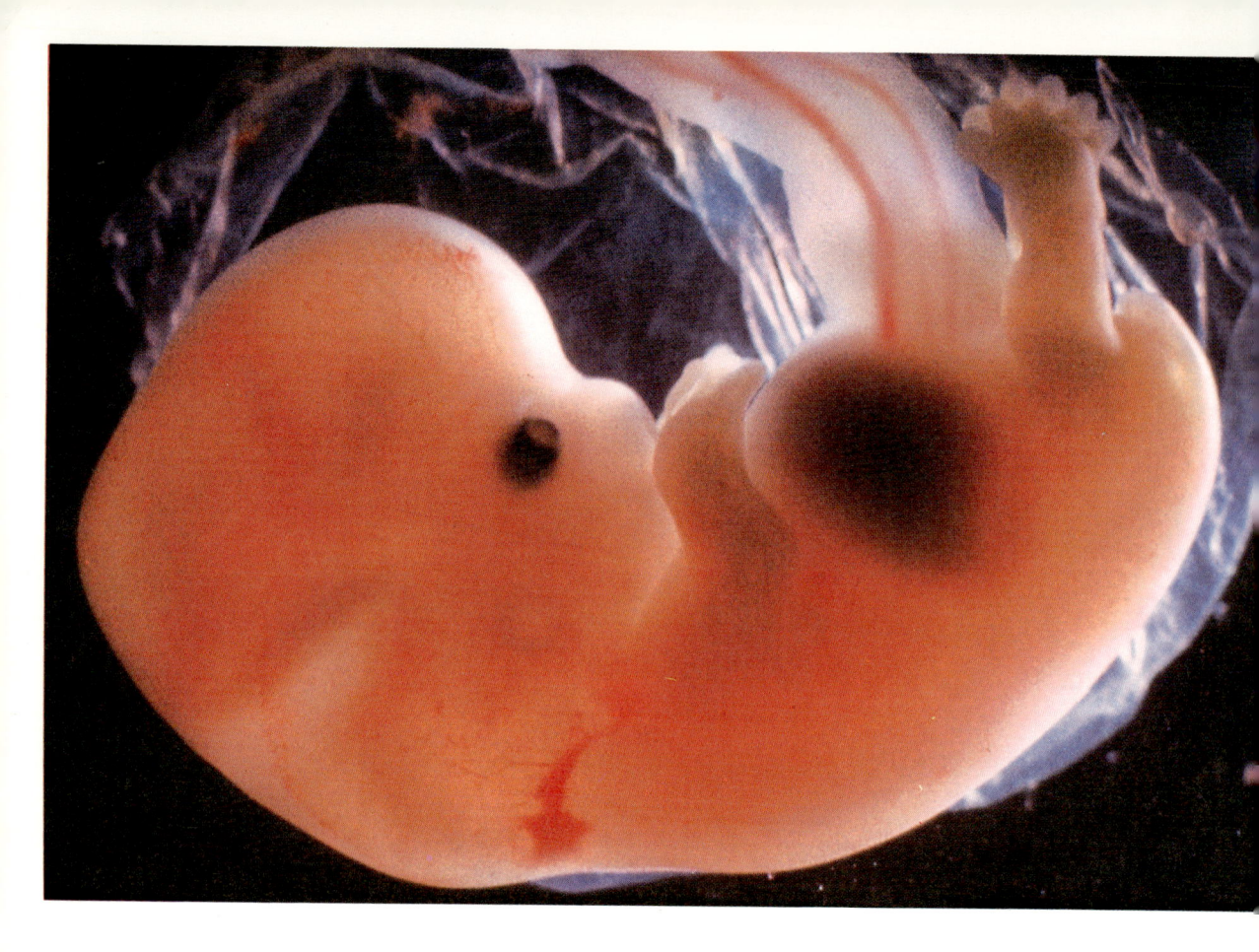

This is a picture of a human embryo inside its mother. Like an astronaut on a lifeline, it floats at the end of the umbilical cord above it. Through this cord, blood and nourishment flow to it from its mother. Seven weeks ago, the embryo did not exist at all. Even by the time its tiny heart began to beat three weeks ago, you could not have seen any difference between it and a mouse or a bird at the same stage. Now it is half the length of your thumb. Five toes are budding on each foot. Eyes and a nose have begun to form. The large dark patch is its liver. Many changes have yet to take place in the next seven months. At the end of that time, a human being will be born.

WITHDRAWN